CRYPTID GUIDES: CREATURES OF FOLKLORE

GUIDE TO Vampires

BY CARRIE GLEASON

CRABTREE
Publishing Company
www.crabtreebooks.com

Developed and produced by Plan B Book Packagers
www.planbbookpackagers.com
Art director: Rosie Gowsell Pattison

Crabtree editor: Ellen Rodger
Crabtree managing editor: Kathy Middleton
Crabtree production coordinator: Katherine Berti
Proofreader: Melissa Boyce

Photographs:
p. 8-9, p. 15, p. 20 (low) Rosie Gowsell Pattison. All other images from
Shutterstock.com.

Library and Archives Canada Cataloguing in Publication
Available at the Library and Archives Canada

Library of Congress Cataloging-in-Publication Data
Available at the Library of Congress

Hardcover: 9781039663473   Paperback: 9781039663961
Ebook (pdf): 9781039668393   Epub: 9781039685796

Crabtree Publishing Company
www.crabtreebooks.com   1-800-387-7650

Printed in the U.S.A./072022/CG20220201

Published in Canada
Crabtree Publishing
616 Welland Ave.
St. Catharines, Ontario
L2M 5V6

Published in the United States
Crabtree Publishing
347 Fifth Ave.
Suite 1402-145
New York, NY 10016

CONTENTS

CRYPTIDS
and
KINFOLK

This chart shows some of the best-known cryptids and creatures from folklore. How many of them do you think are real?

LAND DWELLER

UNDEAD

LIVING

SPIRIT

LIVING CORPSE

HUMANOID

Zombie

Mummy

Werewolf

Werecat

Grim Reaper

Ghoul

Vampire

Bigfoot

Mothman

WHAT IS A VAMPIRE?

A vampire is a creature from folklore. In folkore there are many different types of creatures that are generally believed to be made up, such as werewolves, zombies, elves, and giants. Other creatures from folklore are cryptids, which are animals that may or may not exist, such as Bigfoot or the Loch Ness Monster. The information about vampires in this book comes from folklore from different parts of the world where people once believed in vampires. Could vampires be real? This Cryptid Guide will help you decide!

ANIMAL & HYBRID

Unicorn

Jackalope

Chupacabra

OTHERWORLDLY

GIANT

Fairy

Elf

Nymph

Ogre

Troll

SEA MONSTER

EXTRATERRESTRIAL

SWAMP MONSTER

Mermaid

Sea Serpent

LAKE MONSTER

Alien

Louisiana Swamp Monster

Leviathan

Loch Ness Monster

Ogopogo

Champ

FEAR THE VAMPIRE...

Imagine this: It's long, long ago, before modern medical science has discovered the truth about how germs, diseases, and viruses work. A man in your village has become ill and died. A few days later his daughter swears she saw him at her bedside in the middle of the night. The next day she becomes ill too. One by one, her mother, brother, and sisters all become sick. They all say they saw the father after he died, in the dead of night. What is going on? Why are people reporting to have seen a dead man and then becoming sick and dying? There can be only one explanation—the man returns from the dead each night to infect the living. Are you next? What if the whole village becomes infected? This must be stopped! And the only way to do this is to dig up the dead man's grave and drive a stake through his heart...

VAMPIRE RELATIVES

Zombie

A zombie is a reanimated corpse—a dead body that lacks a soul or spirit but can still move around. It looks like a human because it once was a living, breathing person. Zombies feed on the flesh of the living.

Mummy

A mummy is a dead human whose flesh and organs have been preserved rather than left to rot. Real mummies are found in Egypt and South America. Reanimated mummies and their cursed tombs are the stuff of folklore.

Ghoul

A ghoul is any type of undead creature that feeds on rotting human flesh. They are half human and half demon and can be found lurking around graveyards looking for their next meal.

VAMPIRE BASICS

According to folklore, vampires are humans who return from the dead to drink the blood of the living and turn them into vampires. People around the world have been telling stories of vampires and other bloodsucking monsters for centuries. Nowadays we know vampires aren't real. But at some points in history, people believed in real vampires as a way of making sense of things they couldn't understand, such as how sickness and disease spread. Luckily for vampires, our idea of how they behave and what they look like has changed over time. Thanks to books, TV, and movies, today we're just as likely to fall in love with a vampire as to fear one!

ANATOMY OF A VAMPIRE

Vampires are the lords of darkness that haunt the night. They look similar to living humans, but with some differences. Here's how to spot a vampire.

THE VAMPIRE TEST
How to tell if someone is a vampire

You will need:
• A mirror or a piece of glass
• A suspected vampire

What to do:
Place the mirror or piece of glass in front of your suspected vampire.

What happened?
Observation: There was a reflection
Result: NOT a vampire

Observation: There was no reflection
Result: Vampire

Why?
The idea that a vampire doesn't have a reflection comes from an old belief that mirrors reflect a person's soul. A vampire is believed not to have a soul, and therefore has no reflection. It also means that their picture can't be taken nor can they be captured on video.

May have blood stains around the mouth

Pale skin from lack of sunlight

Body looks just like a human body, but they have super-human strength and speed

Wounds and scratches heal super fast

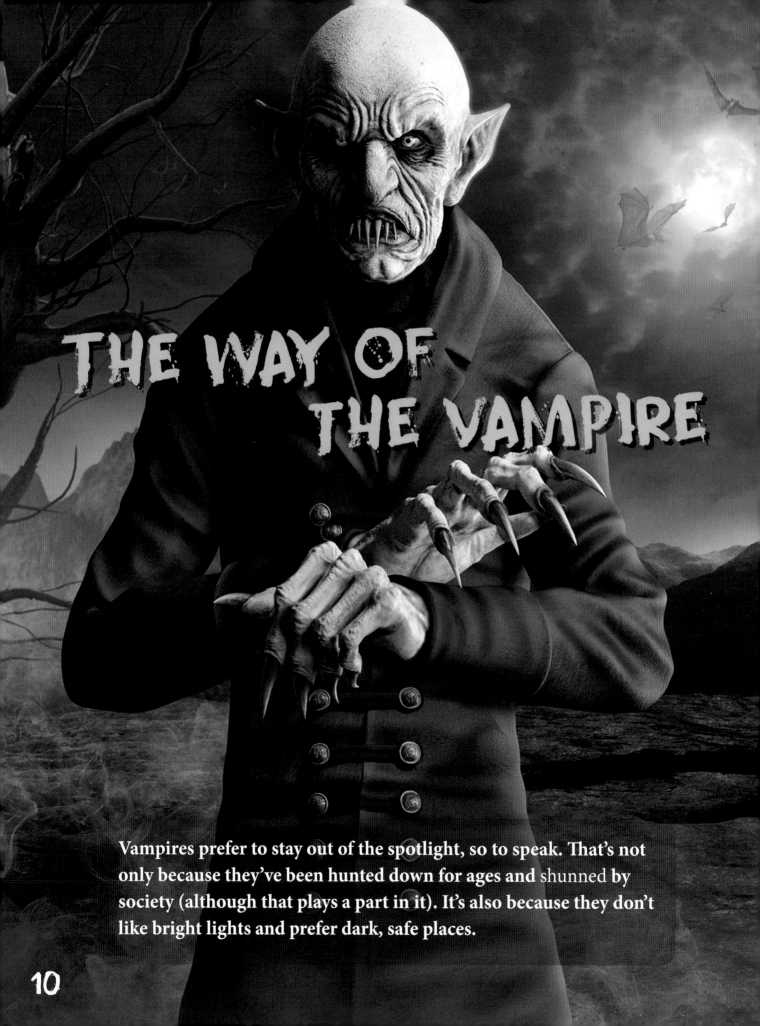

THE WAY OF THE VAMPIRE

Vampires prefer to stay out of the spotlight, so to speak. That's not only because they've been hunted down for ages and shunned by society (although that plays a part in it). It's also because they don't like bright lights and prefer dark, safe places.

SOMEONE MIGHT BE A VAMPIRE IF...

- they like to sleep all day and are active at night
- they will not enter a home unless invited in
- they have a desire to count things
- they have mind-control powers
- they can take the form of a bat, wolf, owl, rat, spider, or a whiff of smoke
- they can fly or crawl up walls
- they feed on blood from both animals and humans by making puncture marks in the necks of their victims with their fangs (this one is a real "dead giveaway")

VAMPIRES DON'T LIKE:

religious objects, such as crosses and rosary beads

garlic

sunlight

silver

SOMEONE MIGHT BECOME A VAMPIRE IF...

- they are bitten by a vampire
- they have been cursed or an evil spirit enters their body after death
- they die from unnatural causes, such as a violent act
- a cat jumps over their grave or they were not properly buried

WHAT TO DO IF YOU HAVE BEEN BITTEN...

- find the vampire's grave and eat some dirt from it

Although often thought to be lonely, vampires do sometimes have friends. A group of vampires is called a hive or a coven.

VAMPIRES AROUND THE WORLD

BEWARE: A FACT!

A mandurugo is a beautiful female bloodsucking vampire from the country of the Philippines. She tricks men into marrying her so she will have a steady supply of blood to drink.

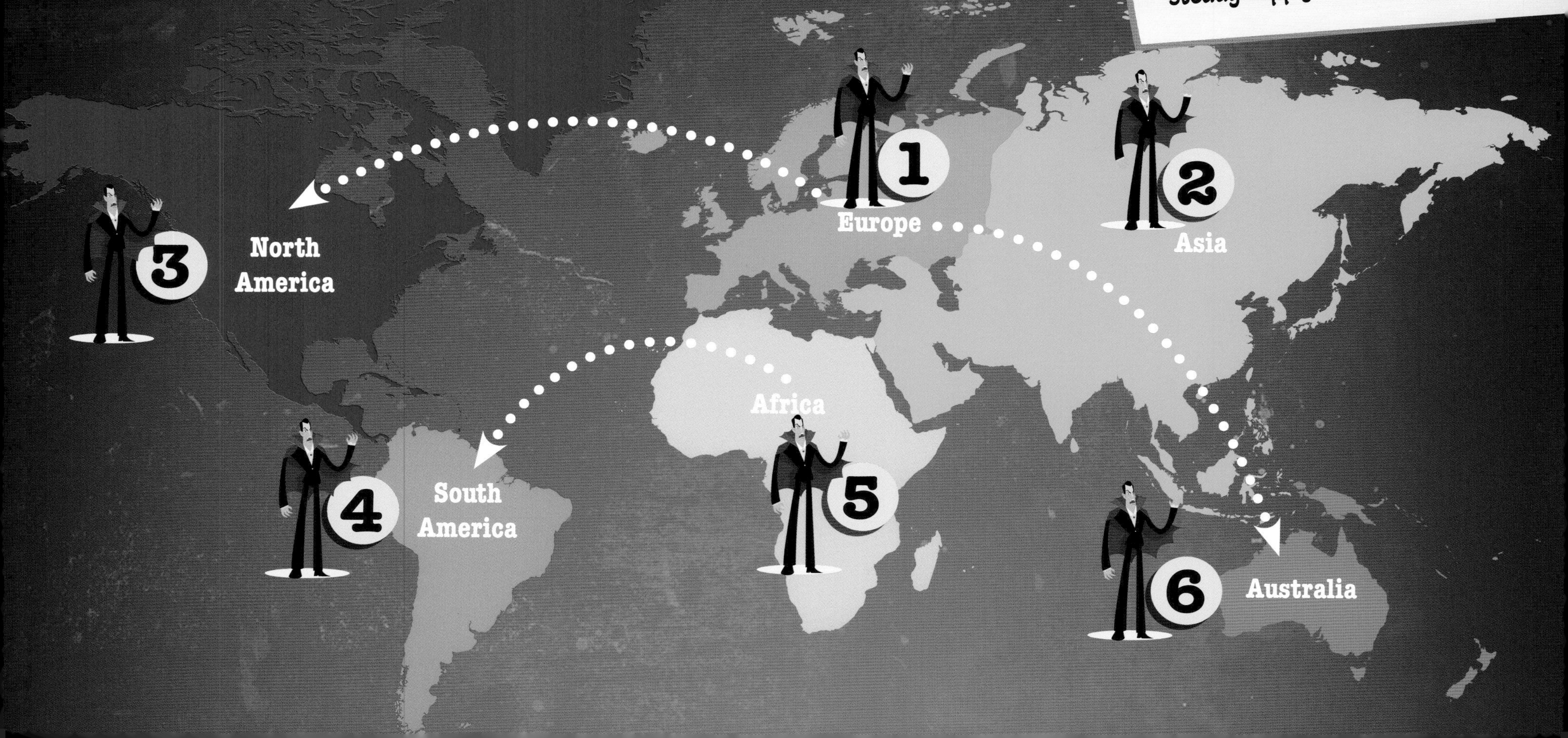

1
Europe
2
Asia
3
North America
4
South America
5
Africa
6
Australia

3

Hollywood movies bring vampires to life in popular films, especially ones that star Count Dracula.

6

Indigenous legends tell of a vampire-like creature from Australia that has the body of a frog with a giant, human-like head.

2

In China, jiangshi are undead creatures that live in graveyards. These stiff vampires can only hop or jump, and instead of drinking blood, they feed on a person's qi—or life source—at night.

5

Witches with vampire-like traits appear in myths and legends from many cultures in Africa.

1

The word "vampire" comes from the Serbian word *vampir*. (Serbia is a country in Eastern Europe.) There are many types of vampires from Eastern Europe, some of which are also witches or werewolves.

4

Tales of vampires from South America come from the vampire-witches of Africa.

VAMPIRES ARE EVERYWHERE!

Our ideas about modern-day vampires are based on folklore and legends from Eastern Europe. But almost every culture around the world has its own version of a vampire-like creature.

13

OTHER BLOODSUCKING CRYPTIDS

Vampires are by the far the best known of the bloodsucking cryptids, but they are not alone in their thirst for blood. Here are some other bloodsucking cryptids from folklore.

BAOBHAN SITH

A baobhan sith is a bloodsucking fairy-vampire from Scottish legends that always wears a green dress. They have deer hooves for feet and, like vampires, are nocturnal. They can change into a raven, a crow, or a wolf. Instead of fangs, they use their fingernails to scratch their victims to get at their blood.

CHUPACABRA

Reports of a chupacabra first surfaced in the 1990s in Puerto Rico. The creature has been described as dog- or lizard-like, with sharp fangs that it uses to drain livestock of their blood. Ideas of what chupacabras are vary from an alien to a top-secret military experiment gone wrong.

YARA-MA-YHA-WHO

A yara-ma-yha-who is a vampire-like creature from Australian legends. It has red skin and is described as a cross between a frog and a human. Although it has a large mouth, it has no teeth, and instead uses suckers on its fingers and toes to drain blood from its victims. The creature perches in tree branches and drops down on victims from above.

LOOGAROO

A loogaroo is a bloodsucking hag from Caribbean folklore. These shapeshifting blue streams of light take the forms of old women during the day by wearing their skin. Old women become loogaroos by making a deal with the Devil, who gives them magic powers in return for providing him with blood. Instead of sucking on necks like vampires, they suck blood from a sleeping person's arms or legs.

BIRTH OF A VAMPIRE

After dying and being buried for a few days, a vampire comes back to life and digs its way out of its grave. Many times in history, graves of people thought to be vampires have been dug up to examine their corpses. Our ideas about what vampires look like come from the appearance of corpses as they decompose, or rot.

FIVE THINGS VAMPIRES AND CORPSES HAVE IN COMMON

1 Long fingernails. Bodies decompose, or rot, as muscle and flesh break down. The idea that vampires have long fingernails is really a case of shrunken fingers. Fingernails don't decompose at the same rate because they are made from hard proteins called keratin and biotin.

2 Pale, waxy-looking skin. Corpses have pale skin because the heart no longer pumps blood around the body. As bodies decompose, gases are created that cause the skin to appear bloated.

3 Fangs. During decomposition, the gums in the mouth dry out, which causes them to shrink back, making teeth look larger. Already pointy incisors appear longer and larger, like fangs.

4 They make sounds. Gases escaping from dead bodies can make it sound like a corpse is moaning.

5 Bloody mouths. After death, internal organs such as the heart and lungs start to break down and turn to liquid. This dark-colored liquid sometimes escapes the body through the nose and mouth, and can easily be mistaken for blood.

VAMPIRE BURIALS

Vampires like to keep dirt from where they were buried in their coffins or crypts—it's kind of like their comfort blankie. In places where people thought vampires were real, they came up with ways to stop vampires from escaping from their graves. Real-life vampire burials included:

- Burying a person facedown, so that they dig the wrong way after coming back to life as a vampire.

- Burying the body with the stems of a wild rosebush, so the sharp thorns would keep it from moving.

- Driving an iron rod through the coffin or a stake through the heart.

- Tying the body up or piling stones on top of the grave to keep the vampire from escaping.

- Scattering grains of rice, seeds, or pebbles around the gravesite. Vampires can't help but stop to count them all!

- Cutting the knee tendons (the tissue that connects the muscle to bone) so that the vampire can't walk.

- Burying the dead with a religious object.

- Burying someone at a crossroads so that the vampire won't know which road to take to get back home.

FACT OR FICTION?
Some people used to believe in vampire babies.

FACT. According to folklore, a baby born with teeth or a strange birthmark may grow up to be a vampire. A baby might also become a vampire if it was born on Christmas Day.

THE UNDEAD

Another word for a creature that is undead or that has returned from the dead is a "revenant." A vampire is a revenant, as is a ghost and a zombie. There are two types of revenants: corporeal and spirit. Not all revenants drink blood like vampires though.

Corporeal
vs
Spirit

Corporeal revenants are reanimated corpses, or dead bodies that are brought back to life. The soul, or spirit, does not return, which means they are not the same person that they were when alive.

Spirit revenants do not have a physical body, although they may have a physical shape. Another way of putting it is that they are the bodiless souls of people who were once alive.

CORPOREAL

ZOMBIES

Zombies come from Haitian folklore. (Haiti is a country in the Caribbean.) Sorcerers or witches called bocors bring these corpses back to life. Zombies have no will of their own and are the bocor's slaves.

SPIRIT

GHOSTS

Ghosts are the spirits of people who have died. Ghosts can be transparent, shadowy figures, human-like figures, whiffs of smoke or fog, or a form of light. Ghosts are said to haunt places that were special to them in life.

CORPOREAL

DRAUGRS

Draugrs come from Norse folklore and legends. They are found around their graves protecting the treasures they were buried with. Draugrs have some special powers, such as the ability to shapeshift and enter the dreams of the living.

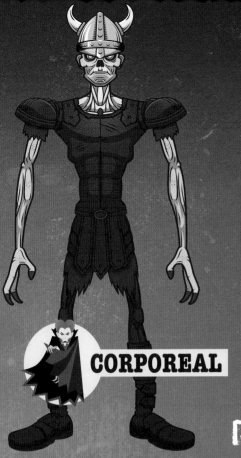

CORPOREAL

NACHZEHRER

A nachzehrer comes from German folklore. It is a cross between a vampire and a ghoul that returns from the dead. A nachzehrer feasts on human flesh or energy for nine years after its death.

SPIRIT

WRAITHS

A wraith comes from Scottish folklore. It is the spirit of a dying person that leaves the body and appears just before, during, and after the time of death. Wraiths do not cause harm.

19

THE LEGENDS BEGIN

Most cultures around the world have myths or legends about vampire-like creatures. These creatures are often supernatural beings such as gods that have special powers. Here are a few myths and legends about vampire-like creatures from long ago.

Myth vs Legend

Myths are stories from the distant past and are known to be untrue. Myths usually involve gods, creation stories, and moral lessons.

Legends are old tales told as if based on experiences of real people. Legends may have started as truth, but by retelling them over and over again, they become more and more exaggerated.

Children beware!

MYTH

In ancient Greek myths, Lamia was a queen of Libya. The powerful god Zeus fell in love with her and they had children together. Zeus's wife, Hera, became jealous and killed Lamia's children. Hera turned Lamia into a monster who roamed around at night drinking the blood of other children.

The Mother of Vampires

MYTH

No one knows the exact beginning of the myth of Lilith. According to Jewish folklore, she was the first wife of Adam. Lilith left the Garden of Eden and went to live with demons, where she had 100 demon children each day. As punishment for not returning to her husband, God killed Lilith's children. Babylonian myths say that Lilith was a female demon who drank people's blood at night.

Blood brothers

LEGEND

According to a Scandinavian legend, Aswid and Asmund made a pact that if one of them died, the other would be buried with him. When Aswid died, Asmund kept his promise and was placed in Aswid's tomb with him. Soon after, Aswid became a draugr. For hundreds of years Asmund fought Aswid every night. One day a group of people opened the tomb, which distracted the draugr long enough for Asmund to finally defeat him.

DANGER: VAMPIRES OF EASTERN EUROPE

UPYR (RUSSIA): These vampires have teeth made of iron and are active in daylight. They drink the blood of whole families—starting with the children!

STRZYGA (POLAND): An undead female witch-vampire that flies at night in the form of an owl, attacking people and sucking their blood.

STRIGOI (ROMANIA): Troubled souls of the dead that rise from the grave. They can transform into animals, become invisible, and drink blood.

VRYKOLAKA (GREECE): Instead of drinking blood, these undead creatures get it from eating the livers of their victims.

VAMPIIR (ESTONIA): Vampires that sneak into people's homes and smother them by lying on top of them while they sleep. They are only active for a short time each night.

KRVOIJAC (BULGARIA): A vampire that has only one nostril and a barbed tongue. It prefers animal to human blood.

IELE (ROMANIA): A cat vampire. They are about 4 feet (1.2 m) tall and feed mostly on sheep's blood.

VAMPIRE PUMPKIN (SERBIA): Pumpkins left in the house longer than 10 days can turn into vampires! They are generally harmless and roll around oozing blood.

VAMPIRE PANIC

In the 1700s, panic about real vampires spread across Eastern Europe to other parts of Europe and eventually to North America. People suspected of being vampires had their graves dug up and their heads cut off. A stake was driven through their hearts, or their bodies were burned. Even some official reports and newspapers blamed vampires for the spread of illness.

Date: 1672

Place: **Present-day Croatia**

Name: **Jure Grando**

Facts: In 1656, Jure Grando got sick and died. For 16 years after his death, he was believed to have terrorized his village. People who thought they had seen Jure after his death also fell ill and died.

Result: **Villagers dug up his corpse and beheaded it.**

Date: 1725

Place: **Present-day Serbia**

Name: Petar Blagojevich

Facts: Petar Blagojevich was a farmer. It was believed he returned from the dead as a vampire and killed nine people from his village.

Result: **His body was dug up and burned.**

Place: **Rhode Island, United States**

Name: Sarah Tillinghast

Facts: 19-year-old Sarah died from a disease called tuberculosis. After her death, 5 of her 13 siblings said they saw her. They too got sick and died.

Result: Her grave was dug up, and her heart was cut out of her body and burned.

Date: 1732

Place: **Present-day Serbia**

Name: Arnod Paole

Facts: Arnod Paole was a soldier who died soon after he returned home. People reported seeing him around town after his death, sometimes in the form of a black dog. About 20 people in the village died shortly after seeing him.

Result: Villagers dug up his grave and put a stake through his heart.

Date: 1892

Place: **Rhode Island, United States**

Name: Mercy Brown

Facts: After Mercy died from tuberculosis, it was believed that she had risen as a vampire and was preying on her family.

Result: Her heart and liver were burned and the ashes fed to her brother to protect him from illness.

23

HOW TO STOP A VAMPIRE

Vampires rob people of their blood, their health—even their lives. In the folklore of Eastern Europe, there are almost as many different types of vampire hunters as there are vampires. They are called vampirdzhiya, vampirar, dzhadadzhiya, or svetocher. Each one specializes in killing a different kind of vampire.

In Bulgarian folklore, children who have one parent that is a vampire and the other who is a human are called dhampirs. Dhampirs make excellent vampire hunters because they are the only ones who can see invisible vampires!

VAMPIRE HUNTING 101
STEP 1: PACK YOUR KIT

You will need:

- a cross or other religious object
- holy water (regular water that has been blessed by a leader from a Christian church)
- a stake and mallet
- a crossbow, if you have one

TIP: Splashing a vampire with holy water will make its skin burn, but will not kill it.

STEP 2: FIND A VAMPIRE

- Visit a cemetery and look for finger-sized holes in graves (vampires who can turn into mist come and go from these holes).
- Take a horse to a graveyard. If the horse doesn't walk over a grave, it may belong to a vampire.
- Dig up the grave.

TIP: Vampires are weakest when sleeping, so the best (and safest!) time to hunt a vampire is during the day.

STEP 3: WAYS TO KILL A VAMPIRE

- fire
- beheading
- direct sunlight
- a wooden stake through the heart or mouth
- stuff their mouths with dirt from their graves

TIP: If a vampire starts to hunt you, escape by crossing a river (vampires don't like running water) or by hiding out in a church (vampires can't enter holy places).

THE CRYPTID RECORD

Cryptozoology's #1 Source for Sightings

Bloodthirsty Nobles Unearthed!

Fact or Fiction?

History is filled with stories of rulers known for their cruelty. In Europe, some of these rulers are associated with vampire folklore. People who study history today believe that some of their evil deeds may have been exaggerated by their enemies. Of the four nobles on these pages, only one of them, Count Dracula, is made up—but even he is believed to be based on a real-life ruler, Vlad the Impaler.

Viscount de Morieve
France, 1799

The French nobleman Viscount de Morieve was beheaded for killing people on his estate. Seventy-two years later a wooden stake was driven through his heart by a vampire hunter. The new viscount, de Morieve's grandson, believed his grandfather was a vampire who had killed many children in the village.

Elizabeth Báthory
Hungary, 1610

As punishment for her vampiric crimes, noblewoman Elizabeth Báthory was locked away in a castle. She was found guilty of murdering hundreds of young girls and bathing in their blood, which she believed would keep her young.

Count Dracula, Transylvania, 1893

The fictional character of Count Dracula left his Transylvanian castle and took a ship to England. The 400-year-old Count is described as handsome, with sharp teeth, hairy palms, and long, sharp fingernails. He is also known for his smelly breath and strong mind-control powers.

Vlad the Impaler Romania, 1476

Wallachian prince and former ruler Vlad the Impaler was killed in an ambush while trying to take back his crown from his brother. The Romanian ruler is well-known for impaling his enemies on wooden stakes and leaving them to die. His father was known as "the dracul," which means "the dragon." Despite his crimes, the people of Romania remember him as a hero who protected them from invaders.

VAMPIRES MAKE IT BIG

What do you picture when you think of vampires today? Early vampires from folklore were not the well-dressed, handsome creatures of today. They were ugly and scary monsters. This timeline shows where some of our ideas about modern vampires came from.

1972
The *Sesame Street* character Count von Count is created. The Count is known for his friendliness, his laughter, and his love of counting.

1958
Horror of Dracula, a film starring Christopher Lee as Dracula, is released. Christopher Lee would appear in eight more Dracula movies. He wears a red-and-black cape.

1975
Horror writer Stephen King publishes the book *'Salem's Lot*, about a place in Maine where everyone turns into vampires.

1976
Vampires in the book *Interview with the Vampire* by Anne Rice aren't bothered by crosses or garlic and live among people in New Orleans, Louisiana.

2012
The children's animated movie *Hotel Transylvania* is released. The story follows a vampire father who tries to keep his 118-year-old vampire daughter safe from humans.

2005
The novel *Twilight*, by Stephanie Meyer, is published. Edward Cullen, the vampire in the book, is a 103-year-old vampire in a 17-year-old's body.

1819
The short story "Vampyre" is written for a contest by British author John Polidori. The story of Frankenstein by Mary Shelley was also created for this contest.

1845
"Varney the Vampyre" stories start out as a weekly pamphlet known as a penny dreadful. The vampire in the story, Sir Francis Varney, is the first to have fangs.

1897
Dracula by Bram Stoker is published, giving birth to the most famous vampire ever known, Count Dracula.

1931
The movie *Dracula*, starring actor Bela Lugosi, is released. In the film Dracula has a Hungarian accent.

1922
In Germany, the silent vampire movie *Nosferatu* is made. The vampire, known as Count Orlock or "The Bird of the Dead," is bald and hunched over, with large, pointy ears.

1979
The comedy-horror film *Love at First Bite* is released. It has similar characters to *Dracula*, but is set in modern-day New York City.

1979
Bunnicula is published. It is the first book in a children's novel series about a vampire rabbit that sucks all the juice out of vegetables.

1987
The Lost Boys is released. It is a movie about a group of teenage vampires who are outsiders in their community.

1992
The comedy-horror film *Buffy the Vampire Slayer* is released. Buffy is a teenage cheerleader who fights vampires.

1992
A new hit movie called *Bram Stoker's Dracula* is released. In the film, Dracula no longer wears a cape and his fangs are retractable.

Vampires Explained

Porphyria is a real medical condition that may explain why some people have a vampire-like appearance. Porphyria is a blood disorder that causes the body to produce less heme. This is a part of hemoglobin, the protein in red blood cells that carries oxygen from the lungs to the rest of the body. In fact, porphyria is sometimes referred to as the "vampyre disease."

People who have it:

- are sensitive to sunlight
- have receding gums
- pee blood
- have a sensitivity to garlic because of the sulfur content

Another condition is Renfield's syndrome, which is a **psychiatric** disorder. It is also called clinical vampirism. People who have this disorder have a strong desire to drink blood.

Vampire Animals

Humans aren't the only vampires in folklore. Tales of animals such as dogs and spiders being vampires have also been told. In real life, some animals do drink the blood of other animals. These blood-drinking animals are known as sanguivorous animals. Here are just a few of them.

Leeches

Vampire bats

Mosquitoes

Bedbugs

Lampreys

LEARNING MORE

Want to know more about cryptids, myths, and monsters such as the ones described in this book? Here are some resources to check out while on your cryptid-hunting quest.

Books

Bunnicula: A Rabbit-Tale of Mystery, 40th Anniversary Edition by Deborah Howe and James Howe. Atheneum Books, 2019.

Monster Science: Could Monsters Survive (and Thrive!) in the Real World? by Helaine Becker. Kids Can Press, 2016.

Vampires by Stephen Krensky. Lerner Publishing Group, 2007.

TV and Films

Monstrum is a series of videos created by PBS about monsters, myths, and legends.

Find the videos on the PBS website at:

www.pbs.org/show/monstrum/

Websites

The Centre for Fortean Zoology is a cryptozoology organization that researches cryptids from around the world. They produce a weekly TV show, books, and magazines about cryptids.

www.cfz.org.uk/

GLOSSARY

Babylonian An ancient civilization in the part of the world that is now Iraq, in the Middle East

century One hundred years

folklore The stories, customs, and beliefs that people of a certain place share and pass down through the generations

impaling Piercing an object with something pointy

incisor A type of tooth near the front of the mouth that is sharp and used for cutting

myths Traditional stories and beliefs, usually about gods and other supernatural figures. Together, myths are called mythology.

noble A person of high standing in a society

nocturnal A word that describes something that is active at night rather than during the day

Norse A word that describes something related to Scandinavia, a part of the world made up of the countries Norway, Denmark, and Sweden

numbing agent A substance that makes a body part lose feeling

preserve To keep fresh; the opposite of rot

psychiatric Relating to mental or emotional health in people

reanimated Brought back to life

retractable Able to draw back in

rosary beads Beads used for prayer by some Christians. Christians follow the teachings of Jesus Christ, who they believe is the son of God.

shapeshifting The ability to take a different form or shape

shunned Ignored or rejected

supernatural A force that is beyond normal understanding

traits The characteristics that make something unique

INDEX